D0883295

REAL-LIFE
SCIENTIFIC
ADVENTURES

# SIR EDMUND HILLARY
# EXPLORES
# MOUNT EVEREST

HEATHER MOORE NIVER

**PowerKiDS**
press™

New York

Published in 2019 by The Rosen Publishing Group, Inc.
29 East 21st Street, New York, NY 10010

First Edition

Editor: Theresa Morlock
Book Design: Reann Nye

Photo Credits: Cover, p. 1 Associated Press/AP Images; p. 5 (top) Popperfoto/Getty Images; p. 5 (Sherpa Tenzing Norgay, Edmund Hillary) Baron/Hulton Archive/Getty Images; p. 6 gracethang2/Shutterstock.com; p. 7 (map) JBOY/Shutterstock.com; p. 7 (bottom) GlobalTravelPro/Shutterstock.com; p. 9 (top) https://commons.wikimedia.org/wiki/File:Mueller_Hut_and_the_summit_of_Mount_Ollivier.jpg; p. 9 (bottom) https://commons.wikimedia.org/wiki/File:View_from_the_summit_of_Mount_Ollivier.jpg; p. 11 (top) Bettmann/Getty Images; p.11 (bottom) Tobin Akehurst/Shutterstock.com; p. 12 Central Press/Hulton Archive/Getty Images; p. 13 (top) Dmitry Pichugin/Shutterstock.com; pp. 13 (bottom), 19 Keystone/Hulton Archive/Getty Images; p. 15 Stringer/AFP/Getty Images; p. 16 PA Images/Getty Images; p. 17 Keystone-France/Gamma-Keystone/Getty Images; p. 18 Arsgera/Shutterstock.com; p. 21 (top) STR/AFP/Getty Images; p. 21 (bottom) AFP/Getty Images; p. 23 Universal History Archive/Universal Images Group/Getty Images; p. 24 L. Blandford/Hulton Archive/Getty Images; p. 25 (top) Mondadori Portfolio/Getty Images; p. 25 (bottom) Lee/Hulton Archive/Getty Images; p. 27 (top) Michael Lewis/Corbis Historical/Getty Images; p. 27 (bottom) https://en.wikipedia.org/wiki/File:Edmund_Hillary_and_Tenzing_Norgay.jpg; p. 28 https://en.wikipedia.org/wiki/File:Junko_Tabei.jpg; p. 29 (top) John van Hasselt/Corbis Historical/Getty Images; p. 29 (bottom) Hulton Archive/Getty Images.

Library of Congress Cataloging-in-Publication Data

Names: Moore Niver, Heather, author.
Title: Sir Edmund Hillary explores Mount Everest / Heather Moore Niver.
Description: New York : PowerKids Press, [2019] | Series: Real-Life
   Scientific Adventures | Includes index.
Identifiers: LCCN 2018000419| ISBN 9781508168621 (Library bound) | ISBN
   9781508168645 (Paperback) | ISBN 9781508168652 (6 pack)
Subjects: LCSH: Hillary, Edmund, 1919-2008–Juvenile literature. |
   Mountaineers–New Zealand–Biography–Juvenile literature. |
   Mountaineers–Everest, Mount (China and Nepal)–Biography–Juvenile
   literature.
Classification: LCC GV199.92.H54 N58 2018 | DDC 796.522092 [B] –dc23
LC record available at https://lccn.loc.gov/2018000419

Manufactured in the United States of America

CPSIA Compliance Information: Batch #CS18PK: For Further Information contact Rosen Publishing, New York, New York at 1-800-237-9932

# CONTENTS

# IMAGINATION AND ENERGY

Many have tried and many have failed to reach Mount Everest's **summit**, the world's highest peak. Everest, which is part of the Himalayas, is located on the border of Nepal and Tibet. This peak's dangerous conditions have caused the world's best climbers to turn back before reaching the top. However, on May 29, 1953, Edmund Hillary, an unknown beekeeper from New Zealand, and Tenzing Norgay of Nepal did what no one had been able to accomplish.

Hillary and Tenzing were part of a British expedition to climb Mount Everest. The two men succeeded. The 15 minutes they spent on that snowy summit made mountaineering, or mountain climbing, history. When they returned from the mountains, the public went wild over the shy beekeeper and the **Sherpa**.

## EXPEDITION REPORT

Hillary always remained humble when he spoke about his journey. He said, "The media have classified me as a hero, but I have always recognized myself as being a person of modest abilities. My achievements have resulted from a goodly share of imagination and plenty of energy."

4

Days after their historic feat, newspapers announced the amazing success of Edmund Hillary and Tenzing Norgay.

## NEWS CHRONICLE

No. 33,381      TUESDAY, JUNE 2, 1953      PRICE 1½d.

# THE CROWNING GLORY: EVEREST IS CLIMBED

**THE QUEEN'S DRESS TODAY**
*Back Page*

*Sherpa Tenzing Norgay*

*Sir Edmund Hillary*

# ENTHUSIASM FOR COLD AND SNOW

Edmund Percival Hillary was born on July 20, 1919. He was raised in Auckland, New Zealand. He had an older sister named June and a younger brother, Rex. His father, Percival, was a beekeeper and created

*Auckland, New Zealand*

a newspaper, *Tuakau District News*. His mother, Gertrude, was a teacher.

As a boy, Hillary loved the outdoors. The fields, hills, and creeks offered hours of fun. He loved reading books by adventure writers such as Zane Grey and going to the movies. He was a small, shy boy. But after taking boxing lessons, he became stronger and more sure of himself. At age 16 he went on a school ski trip to Mount Ruapehu. He said, "I returned home in a glow of fiery enthusiasm for the sun and the cold and the snow—especially the snow!"

Auckland

Tasman Sea

North Island

New Zealand

Wellington

Christchurch

South Island

South Pacific Ocean

This is a photograph of Mount Ruapehu, which is located on the North Island of New Zealand.

# FIRST SUMMIT

As a young man, Hillary attended Auckland University College, where he studied math and science. However, his true interest was the outdoors. It wasn't long before he left school. He worked as a beekeeper with his brother and father.

In 1939 Hillary became serious about climbing. That year he climbed his first peak, Mount Ollivier. He said it was "the happiest day I had ever spent."

When World War II began, Hillary didn't join the military right away. At that time, beekeeping was considered a necessary job and beekeepers weren't required to serve in the military. Hillary's father was a pacifist, which meant he didn't believe that war should ever take place. However, by 1944, Hillary convinced his father to let him join the Royal New Zealand Air Force.

# Mount Ollivier

view from the summit of Mount Ollivier

# MEETING HIS MENTOR

Hillary's military training took place in Marlborough, an area in New Zealand with great climbing opportunities. He then was sent to Fiji and the Solomon Islands to begin his military career. He became a **navigator** on flying boats. Soon after he began work in Fiji and the Solomon Islands, Hillary was injured in a boating accident. He was badly burnt and was sent to the Southern Alps in New Zealand to heal.

While in the Southern Alps, Hillary met New Zealand's top climber, Harry Ayres. Ayres was a very well-known professional mountain climbing guide in the Mount Cook region. Ayres became a sort of mentor, or teacher, to Hillary. They would later spend time climbing together. Hillary learned much from Ayres about the "science of snow and ice craft that only experience can teach."

Harry Ayres (left) was a skillful climber, as Hillary (right) said, for "safe but forceful mountaineering." He was a quick but careful mountaineer.

Southern Alps, Hakatere Conservation Park, New Zealand

# THE MOUNTAINS WERE CALLING

As soon as he healed, Hillary got back to climbing. He was very fit, but Hillary needed to learn the **technical** skills of serious mountain climbing. Ayres helped him with this.

Ayres and Hillary climbed many of New Zealand's peaks over the next three years, including Mount Cook/ Aoraki. Their climbs brought Hillary into contact with other major mountaineers of the time, including George Lowe. Hillary and Lowe talked about climbing in the Himalayas, and it wasn't long before the two did so. In 1951, Hillary joined a British scouting expedition on Everest's southern side. After this, he was asked to join a team that hoped to reach the top.

*George Lowe*

Mount Cook/Aoraki is the highest mountain in New Zealand. It's 12,316 feet (3,754 m) tall.

members of the 1953 Everest expedition

# THE CHALLENGES

Many hopeful climbers have died trying to ascend Everest, which is known as the "roof of the world." Even the trip to get to the base of the mountain is challenging. Choosing the right time to climb is key to a mountaineer's success.

The only times an ascent is possible are just before or just after the summer **monsoon**. Other times, the weather makes the trip too dangerous. **Avalanches** often happen when the snow is soft.

Climbing at high **altitudes** takes its toll on the human body. At heights of over 25,000 feet (7,620 m), breathing and **pulse** rates rise. Climbers experience oxygen deprivation, or a lack of enough oxygen, which makes it hard to think clearly. They also face dangers such as **frostbite**.

## EXPEDITION REPORT

In 1999, an expedition led by American Eric Simonson found Mallory's body. Studies show he probably died from a nasty fall, but it's unknown whether or not he reached the summit.

14

In 1924, a British climber named George Mallory (shown here) and his partner, Andrew Irvine, tried to reach the top of Mount Everest. The two men disappeared.

# PREPPING FOR THE CLIMB

Despite the difficulties that lay ahead, Hillary was excited. "We didn't know if it was humanly possible to reach the top of Mount Everest," he said. "And even using oxygen as we were, if we did get to the top, we weren't at all sure whether we wouldn't drop dead."

The climbers trained by spending three weeks climbing nearby mountains. This gave them the chance

*Colonel John Hunt*

## EXPEDITION REPORT

*Colonel John Hunt headed the Everest expedition. There were 350 porters, 20 Sherpas, and 10 climbers in the party. The plan was to make two attempts to reach the top of the mountain. If the first pair of climbers failed, then a different pair would make another attempt.*

This map shows Hillary's planned ascent of Everest. Every part of the expedition to reach the top of Mount Everest had to be carefully planned: the route, supplies, camps, and more.

EVEREST
29,002 ft.

LHOTSE
27,840 ft.

CAMP 7
27,550 ft.

CAMP 6
25,840 ft.

CAMP 5
22,630 ft.

WESTERN CWM

NUPTSE
25,680 ft.

CAMP 4
21,150 ft.

LHO LA

ICE FALL

CAMP 3
19,350 ft.

CAMP 2
18,370 ft.

CAMP 1
17,220 ft.

KHUMBA GLACIER

BASE CAMP

to test different types of oxygen supplies to see which worked best. They planned out a route and had supplies brought in. They pitched camps and set up paths so that **porters** could hike ahead with supplies. This provided food, oxygen, and other **equipment** in various spots up the mountain. They had to plan when to try the ascent, too. The monsoon was coming.

*17*

# FIRST ATTEMPT

Climbers Tom Bourdillon and Charles Evans were the first to try for the summit. Bourdillon had once been president of the Oxford Mountaineering Club. Evans was a brain surgeon.

Their attempt, which took place May 26, 1953, started with some problems. They didn't start out as early in the day as they'd hoped. However, the pair made good time, reaching a spot called the South Summit at 28,700 feet (8,747.8 m). By 1 p.m., they

*Mount Everest*

*George Band, one of the members of the expedition, wrote that Hillary was strong and ready for the climb: "It was his fourth Himalayan expedition in just over two years and he was at the peak of fitness."*

were only 330 feet (100.6 m) from the top! But Evans was exhausted by the difficult climb and their oxygen supply was very low. Even if they made it to the top, they wouldn't have enough oxygen to get back down safely. They turned back.

# FACING THE STEP

Three days later, it was decided that Hillary and Tenzing would be the next to attempt the climb. After an early start, Hillary and Tenzing reached the South Summit by 9 a.m. But they faced a huge challenge: a **spur** of rock that was 40 feet (12.2 m) high!

Hillary used his ice axe to carve steps into the ice to reach the base of the spur. Then he saw a crack "maybe two feet wide, but just large enough to crawl inside, where the ice was breaking away from the rock. I sort of crawled inside that, and then I wriggled and jammed my way up the crack with rock on one side and ice on the other and then finally pulled myself out onto the top of the rock step."

## EXPEDITION REPORT

Hillary felt that it was important to have a good sense of humor, even when things were serious. On a climb you might get stuck in a tent during a storm, he said. "People who can make you laugh under those circumstances are very valuable indeed in an expedition."

Modern climbers face the spur of rock that was one of the last major challenges Hillary and Tenzing faced on their ascent of Mount Everest.

view looking down from the top of the Hillary Step

# ON TOP OF THE WORLD

Hillary had to stay **focused** to make the climb. "I was constantly doing **mental** arithmetic, checking the pressure of the oxygen bottles," he said. "I had to convert that pressure over to the number of liters of oxygen that remained in the bottle, and then work out how many hours or minutes of activity we still had left." Not only did they need to think about getting up to the peak, but they had to have enough supplies to get back down, too.

By 11:30 a.m. they had made it to the top of Everest! There, the two shook hands. Hillary wrote, "With little hope I looked around for some sign that (Mallory and Irvine) had reached the summit, but could see nothing." After 15 minutes they headed back down the mountain.

## EXPEDITION REPORT

On the way down the mountain one time, Hillary jumped on a piece of ice, which broke. He started to fall. A rope tied Hillary and Tenzing together. Thinking fast, Tenzing wrapped the rope around an axe he stuck into the snow. The rope and the axe stopped Hillary's fall.

Hillary took this now-famous photo of
Tenzing just after the two had made history:
they'd reached Mount Everest's summit.

23

# AFTER EVEREST

Reaching the top of Everest was far from the end of Hillary's adventures. In 1955, he led a supply expedition to Antarctica. While there, he and others continued south on tractors. They reached the South Pole on January 4, 1958. Hillary also became one of the first people to ascend Mount Herschel in Antarctica. He continued to be active most of his life. In 1977 he headed the first expedition to travel up the Ganges River by jet boat. Then, he climbed the Himalayas again to reach the river's source.

Hillary wasn't always climbing. In 1953, he married viola player Louise Rose. They had a son, Peter, and two daughters, Sarah and Belinda. Hillary also enjoyed gardening.

*Louise Rose and Edmund Hillary*

In Antarctica, Hillary and his crew became the first party to travel overland to the South Pole since 1912.

Hillary and fellow mountaineer George Lowe plan their route to the South Pole.

# A SECRET REVEALED

Hillary's photo of Tenzing suggests that the Sherpa was the first to stand on Everest's summit. For years, both Hillary and Tenzing refused to say who had been first. "To a mountaineer, it's of no great consequence who actually sets foot first," Hillary said. In a book in 1955, though, Tenzing revealed that it had actually been Hillary.

Hillary's later life focused on the people of the Himalayas. "I built up very close friendships with them and I became concerned about the things that they wanted: schooling and hospitals," he said. He helped build many schools in the region and created the Himalayan Trust, which helped provide for the people of the area.

Hillary died on January 11, 2008. He lived his life unafraid to reach new heights. But he never forgot about the people who made it all possible.

This photograph shows Hillary being welcomed by students in Khumjung, Nepal.

Hillary and Tenzing

# SIR EDMUND'S LEGACY

In 1953, Edmund Hillary was knighted by Queen Elizabeth II. He published an account of the Everest expedition called *The Ascent of Everest* with Sir John Hunt. He later wrote an autobiography called *Nothing Venture, Nothing Win*. He said, "It's not the mountain we conquer, but ourselves."

Hillary's achievement inspired many others to climb Everest, including his son, Peter. As of 2014, 4,042 climbers have made 6,871 ascents of Everest. One in every 10 successful ascents has ended in death. Avalanches are the leading cause of death, and falls are second.

In 1975, Junko Tabei of Japan became the first woman to reach the summit of Everest. In 2010, at age 13, Jordan Romero became the youngest person to reach the top.

*Junko Tabei*

The equipment used by Sir Edmund Hillary when he made it to the top of Everest on May 29, 1953, is on display in a museum in Christchurch, New Zealand.

# Hillary's Journey

**July 20, 1919**
Edmund Hillary is born in Auckland, New Zealand.

**1939**
Hillary reaches the peak of his first mountain.

**1944**
Hillary joins the Royal New Zealand Air Force.

**1946**
Hillary meets climber Harry Ayres.

**1951**
Hillary joins an expedition scouting Everest.

**May 29, 1953**
Hillary and Tenzing Norgay become the first known humans to reach the top of Mount Everest.

**September 3, 1953**
Hillary marries Louise Rose.

**1955–1958**
Hillary leads the New Zealand members of the Commonwealth Trans-Antarctic Expedition.

**January 4, 1958**
Hillary reaches the South Pole.

**1960**
Hillary establishes the Himalayan Trust.

**1977**
Hillary travels up the Ganges River by jet boat.

**January 11, 2008**
Edmund Hillary dies.

# GLOSSARY

**altitude:** Height above a given level.

**avalanche:** A large mass of snow, ice, earth, or rock in fast motion down a mountainside.

**equipment:** Supplies or tools needed for a certain purpose.

**focused:** Having one's attention directed at something specific.

**frostbite:** The freezing of part of the body.

**mental:** Relating to the mind.

**monsoon:** A seasonal change in wind direction resulting in a change in rainfall or snow.

**navigator:** Someone who navigates, or finds the way.

**porter:** A person who carries things for another person.

**pulse:** The movement of blood through a body, caused by the beating of the heart.

**Sherpa:** A Tibetan people living on the high southern slopes of the Himalayas, or a member of that people, known for providing support for foreign trekkers and mountain climbers.

**spur:** A ridge that extends from a mountain.

**summit:** The highest peak of a mountain.

**technical:** Special and practical knowledge of a scientific subject.

# INDEX

# WEBSITES

Due to the changing nature of Internet links, PowerKids Press has developed an online list of websites related to the subject of this book. This site is updated regularly. Please use this link to access the list: www.powerkidslinks.com/rlsa/hillary